THE MOON OF THE
GRAY WOLVES

THE MOON OF THE
GRAY
WOLVES

BY JEAN CRAIGHEAD GEORGE
ILLUSTRATED BY SAL CATALANO

HarperCollins*Publishers*

The illustrations in this book were prepared with mixed media:
acrylic paints, opaque tempera, and pastels on paper board.

The Moon of the Gray Wolves
Text copyright © 1969, 1991 by Jean Craighead George
Illustrations copyright © 1991 by Sal Catalano

Typography by Al Cetta
2   3   4   5   6   7   8   9   10
NEW EDITION

Library of Congress Cataloging-in-Publication Data
George, Jean Craighead, date
    The moon of the gray wolves / Jean Craighead George ;
illustrated by Sal Catalano.—New ed.
        p.   cm. — (The Thirteen moons)
    Includes bibliographical references and index.
    Summary: Describes the experiences of a wolf pack in the Toklat
Pass of Alaska during the November moon.
    ISBN 0-06-022442-8. — ISBN 0-06-022443-6 (lib. bdg.)
    1. Wolves—Juvenile literature.   2. Wolves—Alaska—Juvenile
literature.   [1. Wolves—Alaska.]   I. Catalano, Sal, date,   ill.
II. Title.   III. Series: George, Jean Craighead, date, Thirteen moons
(HarperCollins)
QL795.W8G4   1991   90-38166
599.74'442—dc20   CIP
                                                     AC

THE THIRTEEN MOONS

The Moon of the Owls (JANUARY)

The Moon of the Bears (FEBRUARY)

The Moon of the Salamanders (MARCH)

The Moon of the Chickarees (APRIL)

The Moon of the Monarch Butterflies (MAY)

The Moon of the Fox Pups (JUNE)

The Moon of the Wild Pigs (JULY)

The Moon of the Mountain Lions (AUGUST)

The Moon of the Deer (SEPTEMBER)

The Moon of the Alligators (OCTOBER)

The Moon of the Gray Wolves (NOVEMBER)

The Moon of the Winter Bird (DECEMBER)

The Moon of the Moles (DECEMBER–JANUARY)

Why is this series called The Thirteen Moons?

Each year there are either thirteen full moons or thirteen new moons. This series of books is named in their honor.

Our culture, which bases its calendar year on sun-time, has no names for the thirteen moons. I have named the thirteen lunar months after thirteen North American animals. Primarily night prowlers, these animals, at a particular time of the year in a particular place, do wondrous things. The places are known to you, but the animal moon names are not because I made them up. So that you can place them on our sun calendar, I have identified them with the names of our months. When I ran out of these, I gave the thirteenth moon, the Moon of the Moles, the expandable name December-January.

Fortunately, the animals do not need calendars, for names or no names, sun-time or moon-time, they follow their own inner clocks.

—JEAN CRAIGHEAD GEORGE

SNOW SHOT THROUGH TOKLAT Pass on a wailing wind that twisted trees and tore at rocks. The wind ripped the snowfall from the alpine slopes and plastered it against the steep face of Mount Sheldon in the Alaska Range. These gargantuan mountains of rock and ice spear the sky north of Anchorage and south of the mighty Yukon River. Their peaks and valleys shelter the royalty of North American mammals: the grizzly bear, Dall sheep, moose, elk, caribou, and the magnificent wolf.

In Toklat Pass the moon of November rose in darkness although it was only four o'clock in the afternoon. The sun sets early and rises late. Mount Sheldon would not see the sun until a few hours before noon the next day.

In the faint light of a crescent moon a large black wolf lifted his nose from his warm tail and sniffed the subzero air. He was the leader of the wolf pack of Toklat River, the leader of four other adults and five pups. Snow crystals clung to his magnificent ruff as he got lightly to his feet. He shook himself and trotted into the blasting wind. Head up, eyes squinted, he fought his way to the knoll above his sleeping pack. They were covered with snow and curled like furry knots on this promontory above the Toklat River. Wagging his tail in pleasure, the black wolf studied his team. He could see them well in the dark. Yellow rods in his eyes absorbed the light from the night's clouds, stars, and moon, and reflected it back onto his retina, making sight possible in the night. The scents and gentle breathing of his mate, his pups, and his three adult helpers aided him in seeing his pack quite clearly.

The moon of November would test the pups for their ability to survive. Few would pass. Only the healthiest and most intelligent would live through the first year. The adults could not coddle them now.

From May to November the adult wolves of the Toklat River pack had cared for the pups. Now they were full-grown and must take their chances against slashing caribou and moose hooves, crevasses and avalanches, disease and accidents. They would be shot at by human beings, who competed with them for game and sold their radiant furs. The life of a wolf is hard and dangerous.

Only a hundred years ago gray wolves roamed across Canada, Alaska, and most of the contiguous United States where wildlife flourished. Ill adapted to civilization, they departed for wilder places. Today the only wolves in the lower forty-eight states hide out in the deep wilderness of Michigan and Minnesota. Canada has a healthy number of wolves, as does Alaska, but Alaska sets no limits for hunting them, and in some areas their numbers are declining.

Standing on the knoll in the wind, the black wolf pricked his ears forward. The frozen valley floor crackled with the activity of caribou, the North American cousin of the Eurasian reindeer. A herd of bulls, with their picturesque branching antlers, had come through Toklat Pass during the day. They were bedding down on the flats near the river. Two thousand strong, they had recently left the slopes of Mount McKinley, the tallest of North American mountains, where their food—the grasses, willow, and dwarf birch leaves—was dying in winter's darkness and cold. Beneath the moon that would test the wolf pups, the caribou were on their way to the lichens in the valley of the Yukon River two hundred miles away. The cows and calves would soon be following the bulls to new foods. The moon of November would also be a test for the caribou.

Caribou are wanderers. All year they circle from one food source to the next, eating, mating, and giving birth as they tread their unending route. This herd was a small fraction of the twenty to thirty thousand caribou in Denali National Park. With the coming of November, after circling a range three to four hundred miles in diameter—which would be the distance from New York City to Pittsburgh, Pennsylvania, or from Quebec City to Gaspé in the Province of Quebec—they were back at Toklat River, where they started.

The black wolf threw back his head and howled a melodious song. His mate, the silver wolf and the leader of the females and pups, answered him. When she was done, the vice-president of the pack sang his aria. He was followed by the young female, who had left her family to join the Toklat River pack. Finally, the old wolf sang out. Then all howled in harmony. If one wolf joined another's note, the first would shift to a new note. Each wanted to express himself with his own individual music, particularly in this, the call-to-action song. It was like a

cheer at a football pep rally, "go, win, go." The wolves of Toklat River sang with great exuberance and anticipation this night. They were out on the promontory living the gypsy life of the wolves again.

The five adult wolves had been confined to a small area since the pups were born in May. Except for hunting the river valley, they had remained close to the old family den. It went twelve feet into the hillside and was used year after year by the wolves of Toklat River. Wildflowers brightened its entrance. For two weeks the mother had remained in the den with the pups, for they were born helpless and blind and needed constant care. During this time the black wolf brought his mate food, placing it far down the tunnel where she could reach it without disturbing the pups. Sometimes the father would wait in the tunnel until he heard them whimper. Then he would back out wagging his tail furiously. The other members of the pack would see his "smiling" tail that said the pups were fine

and well and they, too, would wag their tails.

One twilight when the sun had been shining almost all day, the pups stepped cautiously out of the den. The adults pranced and howled at the sight of them. They sniffed their little noses in greeting and wagged their tails joyously. Wolves love their pups.

During the long hours of daylight in June the pups pounced on bobbing flowers, chased Arctic ground squirrels, and played games like king-of-the-hill and tug-of-war with bones. When their mother went hunting, one of the other adults would baby-sit. Wolves never leave their pups unattended.

In early August, when the pups could tear meat, the black wolf led his pack to their summer home. This was another den used year after year, but a simpler one. It was a tunnel in the middle of a vast alpine meadow. Here the pups could hide when they were tired or frightened, and here, high above the valley, the adults could watch for food: caribou, moose, deer, and Dall sheep.

Wolves prey on big game. They take the sick, and the old, and young and, by harvesting these, keep the wild animals in balance with their food supply. When big game is scarce, the wolf will take marmots, ground squirrels, and even rabbits and lemmings. In the scheme of things, however, these little animals are the natural food of the coyote and fox, the smaller members of the Canidae, or dog family.

One September night the black wolf sat down by the summer den, lifted his head, and howled a song of change. It sounded across the peaks and valleys like a plaintive woodwind instrument. When the song ended, the black leader dashed out over the alpine tundra and up the ridges of the mountain. Life at the summer den was over.

That night the air bit cold, the leaves were long gone from the willows, and the grizzly bears and marmots were in their dens. The black wolf ran at the head of his pack, dashing through snow patches, climbing ridges, and chasing across the flats of his vast territory that reached from Mount

Sheldon to and beyond the park boundary—
caribou land. At sunup they ran out on a rocky
promontory and stopped. Wagging their tails,
they scratched out saucer-shaped beds under the
cold stars and lay down to sleep. The nomadic life
of the wolves had begun.

This night in November they were back on that
same promontory, a favorite site of the black
wolf's because he could survey the river valley
from here. He tensed his muscles. A lone caribou,
who had gotten separated from the herd, was
coming through Toklat Pass.

The black wolf planned a strategy to take the
prey.

He was a thousand feet above timberline, the
line where the trees stop growing and the tundra
takes over. In the Alaska Range the timberline
begins a mere 2,500 to 3,000 feet above sea level.
The farther north from the Alaska Range, the
lower the timberline becomes. In the Arctic
Circle, some two hundred miles above the Alaska
Range, there are no trees at all. The ground is

permanently frozen and only grasses and short-rooted herbs survive.

In the black wolf's territory the trees grew along the rivers and streams. The ice and wind had stunted the trees and clipped them short, and so the black wolf could see right over them into Toklat Pass. The caribou was a female. Her antlers were small compared to those of a bull. She walked in comfort in the fierce cold, for the hair of the caribou is partly hollow, forming a dead air space, which is the best insulation known to man or beast.

A pup yipped, the wrong thing to do when a leader is watching prey. The caribou heard and bolted back down the pass.

The black wolf was not perturbed. There would be others. He returned to his pack and was greeted by his mate. He took her muzzle gently in his mouth to say he was the leader of the pack. She licked his cheek and chin to say he was, indeed, the leader. The other adults paid homage to him in the same manner, and as they did so, the needs

of the pack inspired him: food, companionship, and teamwork. He lifted his head and tail above them in the pose of the loving leader. Wolves have many ways of communicating with each other. Posturing, voice, eye contact, and scent are their languages. With these tools they say all that is necessary for wolf life.

The pups ran to their father. His ears twitched fondly. His tail wagged furiously. Their ears and tails went down to say that he was their leader.

For a moment he studied them. They were still floppy and loose. Pack work would be hard on them, especially on the mindless one who had yipped and scared the caribou, and the lanky one who often tripped over his own feet. Only last night, as he had tracked a porcupine out on the frozen river, he had stumbled and slid, nearly falling into a hole made by a moose who had just broken through the thin ice at the river's bend.

The pups bounced and yipped. The leader was enjoying their enthusiasm, but the old wolf was annoyed. To escape them he trotted to the knoll

animal approached, he ran right up to it. He initiated all the games and chases, and he was persistent. He would stick with a job longer than his littermates, whether it was digging a hole or chasing butterflies. He had all the qualities of leadership—fearlessness, initiative, and diligence. He was an intelligent, strong leader, but he depended on his vice-president brother to work with him for success.

The black wolf joined the old wolf on the promontory edge. He sat down and threw back his head as he howled the opening call of the hunt song. His vice-president brother joined him in song, then the pack sang, and the pups yipped. Their voices carried out across the mountains and down through the pass.

The black-and-white magpies sleeping in the spruce trees along the river opened their eyes. They would listen to the wolves this night. The hunt song meant food for them. The ravens in the crags of Toklat Pass heard the song. They lifted their feathers in contentment. Wolf leftovers were also raven delights.

The rock ptarmigans below the promontory wiggled deeper into the snow and then did not move. The last of their summer plumage had molted, and they were as white as the world they lived in and almost impossible to see. The snow-shoe hares who heard the song pressed their ears closer to their heads and burrowed into the snowdrifts. Porcupines climbed higher in the trees along the river, and a pair of foxes sneaked out on a ledge and watched the wolves. Like the ravens and magpies, the foxes enjoyed the scraps of a wolf feast, too.

The black wolf ended the song and plunged off the ledge. The moon of November was upon the land. His pack followed him down the wind-cleared slope where it seemed no life could survive. Yet they passed creatures who live all winter in the snow and cold. Lemmings ran their tunnels, ground squirrels and marmots hibernated beneath the soil, and two snowy owls sat on top of the snow. The black wolf glanced at the owls as

he ran, holding his head high in the manner of the leader. They had come down from the treeless tundra near Point Barrow, where they had hatched in June in a nest on the ground.

In the constant daylight of the Arctic summer the parents of these owls had hunted the abundant lemmings. Millions of the little furry rodents ran through the grass, eating, building nests, breeding, giving birth to thirteen young at a time, who in a few weeks gave birth to thirteen more, who gave birth to thirteen more until there were too many lemmings. They crowded each other, and in doing so they released a chemical into their bloodstream that made them so restless they ran this way and that. The foxes, owls, gulls, weasels, wolves—every creature that eats meat—fed on them until almost all were gone. A few survived to start the cycle again. The young owls, their food depleted by the normal cycles in nature, took off early for their wintering grounds in the Alaska Range. Some of their relatives would go on into Canada and a rare few as far south as Texas. The two passing over Toklat Pass saw the wolves running and flew down onto the snow. They were not above eating wolf leftovers either.

Breaking into a graceful gallop, the black wolf led his pack across the valley. As they leaped a log, the lanky pup stumbled. The black wolf looked back at him, lifted his lips, and snarled in contempt. The pup whimpered and fell in behind the vice-president to copy an expert stride and learn.

Near the river they swerved to avoid the tight tangles of cranberries, rhododendrons, and crowberries, then entered the stubby spruce forest that edged the Toklat River. They ran swiftly although it was dark under the trees and the snow very deep. The pups struggled; the old wolf panted. The black wolf slowed down to accommodate them.

Fur swinging under their bellies, ruffs blowing in the wind, the pack fought their way to the willow and alder trees that grow at the water's edge. Weaving between these, they slipped out

onto the ice and sped off, galloping again. The old wolf had caught his second wind and the pups were free of the deep snow. The night was electric with caribou scent. They ran in silence looking from right to left for a straggler. So perfectly were they moving, one behind another, that when they passed, it looked as if but one wolf had been on the river. All nine had stepped in their leader's tracks.

Their pace was a moderate fifteen miles an hour when the lanky pup stumbled again. The black wolf looked back at him. Diverted, he did not pick up the faint odor of a moose and her calf bedded down in the alders on the shore. She, however, knew the wolves were running and was about to rise and bolt when the black wolf turned his head, missed her scent, and ran on. When the wolves were far down the river, the moose blew air out of her nostrils to tell her big calf all was well. He snorted an answer from the edge of the grove.

On the frozen river the black wolf picked up

the odor of a caribou ahead. This was what he was looking for, a lone animal. The herd was too dangerous to tackle. He glanced at his vice-president and signaled him by eye contact to move out to the left. With another glance he sent his mate to the right. Then he charged. The two outposts charged. The young female and the old wolf followed. The pups ran behind.

The wolves were down to business, and the wild things knew it. The massive wolverine, walking his lonely trail, pulled into a hollow until they passed. The willow ptarmigans that were flocking by the thousands along the river shifted in the dark. Above them sat a gyrfalcon waiting for the sun. All were aware that the wolves were hunting. A great number of lives were tied closely to the lives of the wolves.

The caribou scent led the black wolf off the river ice into the forest. By now he knew much about his quarry, for scent is perhaps the most vivid language of the wolves. The animal was a bull, and odorously old. Like other male caribou at this time of year, he smelled lean. During the breeding season—from mid-September to the end of October—bulls do not eat, and end the period thin and gaunt. This animal was not well. His urine told of functional weakness.

The black wolf signaled his pack to "exert," then led them through deep drifts. They sank to their chests and lost ground. The caribou made headway. He was designed to travel in these conditions. His huge hooves were like snowshoes that held him up on the crust. Sick though he was, he soon left the wolves far behind.

The wolf pack came to the top of a ridge. The male caribou was ahead of them, too far away to catch. The black wolf did not go on. The old wolf and the pups were tired, and—one pup was missing. The mindless one had fallen into a hole in the river. The black wolf and his mate did not go back to look for her. The moon of November was selecting the pups.

The adults made beds on the hilltop. The pups simply fell in the snow and put their noses in their tails. The lanky pup dropped beside his father. The chase had been long and strenous. The black wolf glanced at him. The stumbler might be the next victim of the moon of November.

A few hours before sunup a whistling wind awoke the black wolf. He stretched and slowly got to his feet.

The river valley was bright with red, yellow, green, blue, and violet lights. He looked up. A fountain of color shot up in the sky and fell back. The aurora borealis was crackling over the Yukon River. Charged particles given off by the sun in a solar flare had been trapped some one hundred miles above the North Pole by the Van Allen belt of radiation. Drawn into curtainlike patterns by the Earth's magnetic field, the particles collide with air molecules and become luminous. The black wolf used the light of the aurora to scan the valley. His eyes focused. His ears shot forward. In the willows on the other side of the river a large beast was walking.

He howled urgently. The vice-president and

his silver mate sprung to his side; the old wolf joined them. The lanky pup, sensing the excitement, chased his tail, then fell into line behind his mother, the young female, and the other pups. They flowed down the slope. At the river's edge a flock of juncos beat their wings frantically in the darkness. The birds had nested by the mountain streams in the summer, flocked by the thousands in September, and were now overnighting as they made their way south to prairies, gardens, and fields in Canada and the lower forty-eight states.

The pack paid no attention to the juncos, but a red fox did. A frightened bird lost its footing in the dark and fluttered down to him.

The wolf pack crossed the river at twenty-two miles an hour. Like one streaming beast it shot up the bank and sped into the willows where the caribou was walking. It was a young bull that was weakened by parasites. The black wolf circled. The caribou thundered out into the open, where he could run faster than the wolves.

The black wolf did not try to catch up with the

speeding bull; rather, he set a steady pace that his pack could keep up all night and the next day, if necessary. The caribou, he knew from experience, could not run fast for long. He would dash swiftly, then rest. With each rest, the wolves, who were steadily, relentlessly trotting along, would gain on the prey.

When, at last, the bull was too tired to sprint, the wolves closed in on him.

The black wolf glanced at his mate. She dashed ahead and stood in front of the tired caribou, who turned to run the other way only to face the black wolf. Another command from his leader—and the old wolf charged. He snapped at the caribou's legs. The bull reared and slashed at him with his razor-sharp hooves, narrowly missing a pup. The black wolf rushed for the animal's vulnerable side and signaled his vice-president to close in with him.

Suddenly the lanky pup bolted forward to help his father. He stumbled. The caribou lowered his piercing antlers and charged the pup. Instantly the

black wolf leaped between the pup and the bull and was hooked on the shoulder. With a swing of his powerful neck the buck tossed the wolf through the air. Falling onto the snow, the wolf rolled head over heels, then flipped to his feet. Stunned, he stood still for several minutes. As he got his bearings, he heard the snarl of the kill.

Now there was food for all. The black wolf trotted to the feast.

Some hours later the pack was comfortably full, yet good meat remained. Picking up a portion, the silver wolf carried it to the edge of the forest, dug a hole, and buried it. The young female cached other pieces, and the pups stuffed bits under logs and bushes. Much of the kill still lay on the snow when the pack went off to the promontory to sleep for the day. The white gyrfalcon awoke and sped down Toklat Pass looking for birds.

When the moon set, shortly after sunup, the black wolf licked his bruised shoulder and surveyed his pack. All were asleep but the lanky pup, who was staring devotedly at him. The black wolf wagged his tail and sighed. His pack was splendid. Even the lanky pup was daring, if not perfect. He might live through the winter after all.

The wind blew in strong gusts as the sun—cold, gold, and heatless—came over the mountains and shone down on the sleeping wolves, who were almost entirely covered with wind-blown snow.

The magpies awoke. They shook out their feathers and yawned. One hopped up through the limbs to the top of a spruce. He looked for the signs of the wolf kill he had heard in the night. Unable to locate it, he took to his wings. Flying high, he saw the torn snow, the fur, and the tasty leftovers. He circled down to the kill. Three more magpies joined him; then from twigs and limbs dozens flew down to eat.

Winging to the feast came two ravens. They had seen the magpies and then the kill from a rocky perch on Mount Sheldon. When the ravens

arrived, the magpies flew off and sat some distance from them on the snow. The ravens were the dominant birds at the feast. As at a state dinner, the birds and beasts seat themselves by rank.

A bald eagle soaring high above the pass saw the ravens and magpies on the snow and flew down to the kill. The ravens stepped aside for him, but not very far. A fox family came to the feast

The wolves of Toklat River had provided a banquet for the inhabitants of Toklat Valley.

As the sun reached its low apogee and started down the sky, the black wolf glanced down at the party. He was not possessive about his food. He did not have to be. Other weakened caribou lingered along the river, and the cows and calves would soon be coming through. Above him the hooves of the Dall sheep clanked on the rocks, and moose walked in the willows. Food was abundant for the wolves of Toklat River.

And—four of the five pups had passed the first test of the moon of November.

Bibliography

Clarkson, Ewan. *Wolves*. Milwaukee, Wis.: Raintree Children's Books, 1980.

Fox, Dr. Michael. *The Wolf*. New York: Coward, McCann & Geoghegan, 1973.

George, Jean Craighead. *Julie of the Wolves*. New York: Harper and Row, 1972.

George, Jean Craighead. *The Wounded Wolf*. New York: Harper and Row, 1978.

Hogan, Paula Z. *The Wolf*. Milwaukee, Wis.: Raintree Children's Books, 1979.

Johnson, Sylvia. *Wolf Pack: Tracking Wolves in the Wild*. Minneapolis, Minn.: Lerner Publications, 1985.

Lopez, Barry Holstun. *Of Wolves and Men*. New York: Charles Scribner's Sons, 1978.

McConoughey, Jana. *The Wolves*. Mankato, Minn.: Crestwood House, 1983.

Mcdonald, David. *The Encyclopedia of Mammals*. New York: Facts on File, Inc., 1966.

Mech, David L. *The Wolf*. New York: The Natural History Press, 1970.

Pringle, Laurence P. *Wolfman: Exploring the World of Wolves*. New York: Charles Scribner's Sons, 1983.

D.E.R

This book is dedicated to Patricia Rose Ray, who could have watched cats for days, and to Louis, who needs to go to sleep now.

The Little Mouse Santi, First Edition

Published in the Confetti Park™ workshop, Bienville Ray, LLC, New Orleans
Text © 2014, David Eugene Ray
Illustrations © 2014, Santiago Germano
Edited by Kathryn Hobgood Ray

For information, visit www.confettipark.com

Library of Congress control number: 2014912441
ISBN: 978-0-692-25225-3

Printed in China.

THE LITTLE MOUSE SANTI

Once there was a little mouse named Santi, whose only desire was to be a cat.

Every day Santi practiced being a cat.

He would practice strutting across the floor, swishing his tail.

He would practice taking cat baths.

MEEOOWWW

He would practice his meows all day and all night.

He would practice ignoring everyone.

He would pretend he was bored.

All the other mice laughed at Santi.

But he didn't care... he knew he would be a fine cat someday.

From his little mousey hole Santi would watch all the cats on the farm and wish he could be with them.

He wanted to be drinking the cream the farmer gave them after he milked the cows.

He wished he could be with them taking naps in the summer sun.

He wanted to be with them chasing bugs in the tall grass in the green fields.

He wished he could be in the lap of the farmer's wife and have her scratch behind his ears.

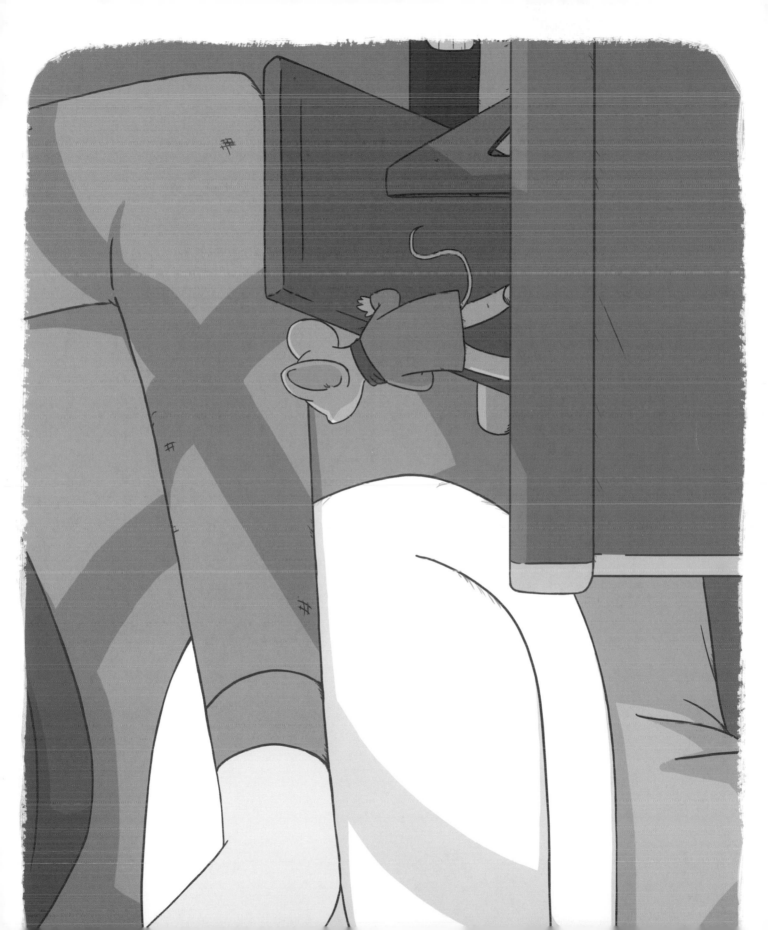

One day Santi decided he was ready ...

... today was the day he was going to become a cat!

But he was afraid... what if the cats laughed at him, too?
What would he do?

Then he noticed one of the cats, a big beautiful orange cat, sitting in the grass by himself.

Santi thought this would be his chance to become a cat.

He would make friends with this cat, who would then introduce him to all the other cats.

o the little mouse, even though he was very scared,
ed his very best kitty strut to approach the orange
at.

When he got there, he sat down and started taking a bath, pretending to ignore the orange cat.

And the orange cat ignored him....
"This is good," thought Santi. "He thinks I'm a cat."

So the little mouse continued taking his bath and continued to pretend to ignore the orange cat.

Santi was happy.

After a while he couldn't stand it any longer. He had to talk to the cat!

He looked at his big orange friend and asked,
"Do you think I make a good cat?"

The orange cat looked at Santi and said,
"How would I know? I'm a dog."

The cat scratched behind his ear with his back leg, and then he walked away.

David Eugene Ray

Was born in Shreveport, Louisiana and spent most of his life rambling, including a stint in the U.S. Navy and years playing music and Ultimate Frisbee. He has a B.A. in history from Tulane University and among other things he has been a school teacher and an educator of the life aquatic.

Nowadays, Dave lives in New Orleans with his wife Kathryn, their son Louis, and their three cats. (No mice—that they know of.) They regularly costume as a family and make wonderful fools of themselves. You can follow Dave's tweets from @aquarium_dave.

Santiago Germano

Was born in Montevideo, Uruguay. As a child, he was inspired to draw everywhere, imagining stories and bringing them to motion. In the following years, he studied illustration techniques and character design. He graduated as a Technical Digital Animator (CRT University). He started to work in games, movies, short films, TV series and children's books a few years ago.

Nowadays, Santiago spends most of his time doing what he loves most, drawing and telling stories with his art.

www.sgermano.com

The End